The MAILBOX®

The Education Center®

W9-ABB-123

Preschool FUN Days

Liven up your lesson plans with superfun single-day celebrations!

- Group activities
- Center activities
- Songs and rhymes
- Art experiences
- Movement activities
- Storytime suggestions
- Snacktime ideas
- Transition tips
- and more!

30 fun themes!

Managing Editor: Kimberly Ann Brugger

Editorial Team: Becky S. Andrews, Lisa Arcos, Diane Badden, Sarah Berkey, Andrea Bourne, Janet Boyce, Amy Brinton, Tricia Kylene Brown, Kimberley Bruck, Karen A. Brudnak, Ann Bruehler, Marianne Cerra, Cari Charron, Julie Christensen, Deb Coman, Clare Cox, Pam Crane, Margaret Cromwell, Chris Curry, Kathryn Davenport, Mary J. Davis, Roxanne LaBell Dearman, Brenda Fay, Pierce Foster, Karen Guess, Tazmen Hansen, Kim Harker, Erica Haver, Kathy Havranek, Marsha Heim, Lori Z. Henry, Kish Jefferson, Amy Lange, Cindy Laskowsky, Kitty Lowrance, Shayne Madison, Coramarie Marinan, Naomi McCall, Caitlin Meadows, Suzanne Moore, Doria Owen, Debbi Pacetti, Tina Petersen, Mark Rainey, Greg D. Rieves, Ashley Rives, Hope Rodgers-Medina, Mary Lou Rodriguez, Deborah J. Ryan, Keely Saunders, Rebecca Saunders, Lisa Shroyer, Donna K. Teal, Mary Tracy, Jan Trautman, Sharon M. Tresino, Christine Vohs, Melissa Voorhees, Carole Watkins, Michelle Weiler, Zane Williard, Ruth Zabelin

www.themailbox.com

©2012 The Mailbox® Books
All rights reserved.
ISBN 978-1-61276-212-8

Printed in the United States
10 9 8 7 6 5 4 3 2 1

HPS233468

Table of Contents

What's Inside

30 fun themes

More than 400 activities and tips

30 timesaving patterns and reproducibles

Plan Your Own FUN Day!

Theme: _____   Date: _____

Circle Time	Movement	Center Time

Snacktime	Songs and Rhymes	Storytime

Art	Transition	Other

 Preschool Fun Days • ©The Mailbox® Books • TEC61354

Theme-for-the-Day
FUN Day!

On _____, _____,
                 day   date

we are having a Fun Day. Our theme for the day will be

_____ .

On this date, you may wish to

☐   add to the fun by dressing your child in _____

_____

☐   send your child to school with _____

_____

☐   join in on the fun! For details, please contact me

_____

☐

_____

_____

Thank you!

Preschool Fun Days • ©The Mailbox® Books • TEC61354

Note to the teacher: Program a copy of the form with the day, date, and theme of your upcoming Fun Day. To make special requests for the day, check any of the provided boxes and supply the necessary details. To make another request, simply check the final box and provide the information. Then sign the copy. Send a copy of the completed form home with each child.

Backward Day

Z, Y, X, W, V, U, T...

Circle Time

○ Read aloud *Brown Bear, Brown Bear, What Do You See?* by Bill Martin Jr. and Eric Carle. Encourage students to chant the text with you. Then read the book aloud again, this time going from the end to the beginning. Challenge youngsters to name each animal that appears in the story, only this time in reverse!

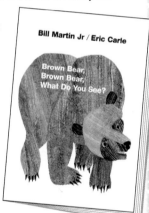

Bill Martin Jr / Eric Carle

Brown Bear, Brown Bear, What Do You See?

○ Display a set of alphabet cards in reverse order. Lead the group in singing the "Alphabet Song," replacing the last line with "Lets all say them backward, please!" Then point to each card, leading little ones in reciting the alphabet from *Z* to *A*!

○ Have children sit in a circle with their backs facing inward! Then announce each letter of the alphabet, beginning with the letter *Z*. When a child's name begins with the specified letter, prompt him to turn and face inward.

Center Time

○ **Writing:** Set out a tabletop mirror. A child draws a picture and writes her name. Then she holds the paper in front of the mirror and examines the reverse images in the reflection.

○ **Games:** Make two tape lines several feet apart on the floor. Put a few toy vehicles on one line. A different student kneels near each vehicle. In unison, the students say, "Three, two, one, it's backward fun!" Then each child crawls backward with his vehicle, saying "Beep! Beep! Beep!" until he reaches the opposite line.

Songs and More

○ Rev Up in Reverse ○
(sung to the tune of "A Tisket, a Tasket")

A tisket, a tasket,
Backward Day's fantastic!
It's fun to do things in reverse.
Let's all have fun and try it!

○ Moving Backward! ○
(sung to the tune of "Good Night, Ladies")

Let's [walk] backward.
Let's [walk] backward.
Let's [walk] backward.
It's so much fun to do!

Continue with the following: *march, crawl, tiptoe*

Snacktime

○ Give each child one slice of bread. Have her roll the bread into a cylinder shape and then wrap a slice of cheese or deli meat around the bread. This backward sandwich is neat to eat!

Art

○ Set out containers of colorful paint and a paintbrush for each container. Give each child a sheet of paper and encourage her to paint a picture using the brush handle instead of the bristles!

Movement

○ Place several plastic hoops side by side on the floor. Invite youngsters to maneuver backward through the hoops, using gross-motor movements such as stepping, hopping, and tiptoeing.

○ For this backward version of musical chairs, have little ones walk around the circle of chairs in silence. Then, when you start a musical recording, have them sit down!

○ Invite pairs of children to stand back-to-back and link arms. On your signal, have each pair walk (one forward and one backward) to a location a short distance away. Then prompt them to walk back in the same manner, with the child who walked forward walking backward.

Transition

○ To transition from circle time, choose a child to begin a countdown. Have youngsters count down from ten to zero around the circle. The child who says "zero" moves to the next activity. Continue until all children have transitioned.

Dear Family,

   Today was **Backward Day**, and we celebrated with lots of fun backward activities! We ate a backward snack, played backward games, read a story backward, and much more. If you'd like, try a backward family activity of your own. Then send a note with your child telling what your family did. We'd love to share your idea at circle time!

   Looking forward to hearing your backward idea!

   _____

Dear Family,

   Today was **Backward Day**, and we celebrated with lots of fun backward activities! We ate a backward snack, played backward games, read a story backward, and much more. If you'd like, try a backward family activity of your own. Then send a note with your child telling what your family did. We'd love to share your idea at circle time!

   Looking forward to hearing your backward idea!

   _____

Preschool Fun Days • ©The Mailbox® Books • TEC61354

Note to the teacher: After your Backward Day celebration, send a copy of this note home with each child.

Beach Day

Circle Time

○ Spread several beach towels on the floor. Play lively summertime music and encourage little ones to dance around the towels pretending to be at a beach party. Stop the music, signaling each child to sit on the nearest towel. Repeat for several rounds.

○ With students watching, place a shell under one of three sand pails (or opaque cups). Direct youngsters to closely watch as you switch the pails. Then invite little ones to tell which pail the shell is under.

Center Time

○ **Water Table:** Place near the table a variety of beach-related sink and float items, such as assorted seashells, sunglasses, toy fish, flip-flops, rocks, and sand toys. A child experiments with the items to see which ones sink and which ones float!

○ **Play Dough:** Set out vinyl placemats or laminated blue paper (ocean) along with colorful play dough and ocean-related cookie cutters. A youngster uses the items to create an ocean scene.

○ **Blocks:** Provide plastic sand pails, shovels, seashells, and small flags. A student engages in pretend beach play, using the props and blocks to build and embellish faux sand castles.

Songs and More

○ A Great Day! ○
(sung to the tune of "Clementine")

We are on the sandy beach,
And we are having so much fun.
Laughing, splashing, waves are crashing,
What a great day in the sun!

For added fun: Use a spray bottle to lightly spritz water on youngsters while singing the third line of the song!

○ Five Little Fish ○

Recite this adorable chant five times, inserting the appropriate number and verb where indicated.

[Five] little fish [are] swimming happily   *Show [five] fingers; move hand in swimming motion.*
Out in the waves of the deep blue sea.
One little fish went to see what it could see.   *"Swim" hand away.*
Now [four] little fish [are] swimming happily.   *Hold up [four] fingers.*

Art

○ Provide ocean critter sand toys (or tracers), paper, crayons, sand, and glue. A child traces critters onto a sheet of paper and colors the tracings. Then she spreads glue around the tracings and sprinkles sand on the glue.

○ Set out shallow containers of paint and a mini beach ball for each paint color. Invite little ones to dip each beach ball in paint and stamp it on a sheet of paper.

Movement

○ Place blue bulletin board paper on the floor so it resembles the ocean. Pretend to be a lifeguard. Encourage youngsters to "swim" and "splash" in the ocean. Then call out, "Shark! Shark! Get out of the water!" prompting little ones to quickly exit the water. Repeat the activity several times.

○ Have children hold the edge of a parachute (or bedsheet). Place one or more beach balls on the parachute and have youngsters make "waves" to toss the ball into the air.

○ Demonstrate swimming motions such as the doggie paddle, breaststroke, sidestroke, and backstroke. Have students practice the motions and then lead them in a game of Lifeguard Says.

Lifeguard says doggie paddle!

Storytime

- *Beach Day*
  by Karen Roosa

- *Sea, Sand, Me!*
  by Patricia Hubbell

- *Curious George Goes to the Beach*
  by Margret and H. A. Rey

Transitions

- Use beach props to transition students from one activity to another! Prompt a child when it's her turn to transition by tossing her a beach ball, lightly tapping her with a pool noodle, or placing a sand pail on her head! You're sure to hear lots of giggles!

- Have little ones walk sideways like a crab as they line up or move to a center.

- Have students pretend to swim as they transition to the next activity.

Snacktime

- Have each child crush a graham cracker in a resealable plastic bag and then put the crumbs in a clear plastic cup. Encourage him to spoon blue-tinted vanilla pudding atop the crumbs and then partially insert a few teddy grahams into the pudding. Those teddies are going for a swim!

More Fun

- Create a reading area with beach towels, handheld fans, sunglasses, and a cooler stocked with beach-related books.

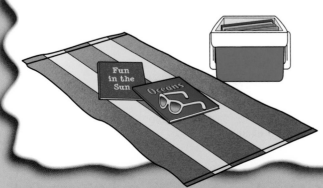

- Using a beach ball, engage students in a game of mock beach volleyball.

- During naptime, play a recording of soothing ocean sounds.

- On occasion throughout your beach day celebration, call out, "Hot sand!" signaling little ones to hop around as if they were walking on hot sand. Then say, "Cool sand!" and have students resume their activities.

Bubble Day

Circle Time

◯ Chant, "Bubbles, bubbles in the sky—how many bubbles floating by?" Then display a number card. Have children identify the number; then count and clap that many times to pop the bubbles!

◯ Ask, "Where would you see bubbles?" prompting answers like a bubble bath, washing hands, and bathing a pet. Record youngsters' responses on paper circles (bubbles) and display them with the title "Bubbles, Bubbles Everywhere!"

Bubbles, Bubbles Everywhere!

◯ in a bubble bath

◯ washing my hands

◯ giving the dog a bath

Center Time

◯ **Discovery:** Fill one-fourth of a resealable plastic bag with water; then add dish detergent. Squeeze out the air, seal the bag, and reinforce the seal with packing tape. A child squishes and shakes the bag, creating a bag full of bubbles!

◯ **Sensory:** Put small sections of Bubble Wrap cushioning material near a tub of water. A student uses her pincer grasp to pop bubbles above and in the water, observing and comparing the feeling and sounds.

◯ **Water table:** Provide bars of hypoallergenic soap and assorted sponges. A youngster uses the soap and sponges to create lots of bubbly lather.

◯ **Math:** Set out graduated size circles (bubbles) cut from Bubble Wrap cushioning material or tagboard. A child arranges the bubbles by size. Then he pretends to pop each bubble, correlating the loudness of the popping sound he makes to each bubble's size!

◯ See page 14 for a reproducible that targets fine-motor skills!

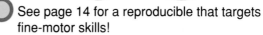

Songs and More

Did You Ever See a Bubble?

(sung to the tune of "Did You Ever See a Lassie?")

Did you ever see a bubble, a bubble, a bubble,
Did you ever see a bubble float this way and that?
Float this way and that way.
Float this way and that way.
Did you ever see a bubble float this way and that?

Bubbles All Around

Bubbles, bubbles everywhere,
Bubbles floating through the air.
Bubbles drifting to the ground.
Bubbles, bubbles all around!

Snack

Give each child a small cup of milk with a straw and several circular cookies. Encourage youngsters to blow through the straw to make bubbles in the milk. Then have them dip their cookies in the milk. Fun and tasty!

Art

Tint containers of bubble solution with bright food coloring. Then encourage each youngster to blow bubbles onto a sheet of white paper and observe what happens when they pop.

Set out plastic bottles and jars and a shallow container of paint. Give each child a sheet of paper. Encourage her to dip the openings of different bottles in the paint and press them on the paper to make prints that resemble bubbles.

Movement

Have children stand in a close circle holding hands. Then ask them to pretend they are blowing an enormous bubble! Direct them to slowly step back as they blow, making the bubble bigger. Then clap your hands and say, "Pop!" prompting youngsters to release hands and fall to the floor.

Put on a recording of music and blow bubbles. Encourage little ones to pop the bubbles as they dance. Have a helper stop the music, signaling youngsters to freeze. After all the bubbles are popped or float away, restart the music and repeat the activity.

Transition

Have youngsters pretend to be bubbles gently floating in the air. Lightly tap each child and say, "Pop!" prompting her to line up or move to the next activity.

To help little ones walk quietly in line, have each child pretend he's holding a bubble in his mouth. Upon reaching your destination, instruct students to release their bubbles!

More Fun

At the conclusion of Bubble Day, give each youngster a small bottle of bubble solution to take home!

Blowing Bubbles

Note to the teacher: Have each child draw circles (bubbles) above the turtles on a copy of this page. Then have him color the page as desired.

Circus Day

Circle Time

○ Secretly think of an animal, a performer, or a food typically found at a circus. Then give clues leading students to guess your secret thought. When your thought is guessed, have each child nibble on an animal-shaped cracker treat!

○ Place three toy hoops on the floor. Invite a different child to stand in each hoop; then whisper the same circus animal name to each child. Role-play the ringmaster and prompt the youngsters to mimic the animal. Signal them to stop, and then ask the group to guess the animal.

Center Time

○ **Play Dough:** Place plastic lids (circus rings) at the center. A youngster molds performers and animals from the dough. Then he pretends his creations are performing in a circus ring!

○ **Fine Motor:** Provide a tube sock, an empty pail, and a pail filled with packing peanuts. A child slides her arm into the sock and pretends it's an elephant's trunk. Then she picks up each peanut and drops it in the empty pail.

○ **Blocks:** Put toy circus animals and empty containers at the center. A student uses blocks and containers to build a railroad track and train. Then he loads the animals onto the train and pretends they are traveling to the circus.

○ **Dramatic Play:** Supply suit jackets, big shoes, feather boas, bow ties, and red sticky dots (clown noses). A child dresses in desired items and pretends to be a circus clown.

Songs and More

● The Circus Is in Town ●

(sung to the tune of "The Farmer in the Dell")

The circus is in town.
The circus is in town,
With [elephants] and acrobats
And lots of silly clowns!

Continue with the following: *lions, tigers, monkeys, bears, seals*

● The Big Top ●

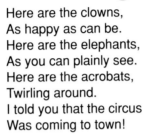

Here are the clowns,	*Frame face with hands and smile.*
As happy as can be.	
Here are the elephants,	*Hang arms low, fold hands, and sway.*
As you can plainly see.	
Here are the acrobats,	*Clasp hands above head; spin around.*
Twirling around.	
I told you that the circus	*Shake finger.*
Was coming to town!	

Art

○ Circus Day isn't complete without cotton candy! To make a cotton candy craft, add a few drops of red food coloring to a mixture of shaving cream and white glue so the mixture turns pink. Glue a cone cutout to a sheet of paper and then add dollops of the mixture above the cone. Allow several days to dry.

Movement

○ Attach a length of tape to the floor. Provide a yard stick or gift wrap tube. Invite little ones to pretend they are walking across a tightrope with a balancing pole. Encourage them to walk heel-to-toe, backward, and sideways.

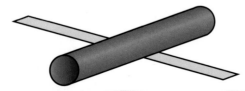

○ Have students (seals) kneel in a circle. Toss a ball to a seal. When it is caught, encourage all the other seals to bark and clap their "flippers." Continue in the same way.

○ Obtain a parachute (circus tent). Announce the names of several students; then call out the name of a circus animal. Have the group lift the tent in the air. The chosen students run underneath mimicking the animal, and then run back to their spots.

Snacktime

○ Help each child spread a thick layer of whipped cream cheese on a rice cake (circus ring). Have her sprinkle graham cracker crumbs or granola atop the cream cheese and then stand animal-shaped crackers in the topping.

Storytime

○ *Clifford at the Circus* by Norman Bridwell

○ *Olivia Saves the Circus* by Ian Falconer

○ *Circus* by Lois Ehlert

Transitions

○ Settle little ones in for naptime with this cute fingerplay.

Here is the circus tent With stripes red and white.	*Press fingertips together forming a tent shape.*
Here are the clowns— What a silly sight!	*Wiggle fingers like clowns running around.*
Under the big top, A day filled with fun.	*Press fingertips together forming a tent shape.*
It's time to rest now. The day is done.	*Pretend to yawn.* *Quietly settle in to rest.*

More Fun

○ Post a large drawing of a clown, minus the nose. Cover a child's eyes with a sleep mask or scarf. Then hand him a red tagboard circle (nose) with rolled tape attached and encourage him to stick the nose on the clown.

○ Provide items, such as small foam balls or beanbags, and invite little ones to perform a juggling act!

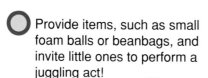

○ Drape a parachute over a table (circus tent). Ask a youngster to leave the area while a classmate hides in the tent. Summon the youngster back to the area and prompt the hidden child to say "Welcome to the big top!" Then encourage the youngster to guess who's in the tent.

Welcome to the big top!

Cookie Day

Circle Time

○ Have youngsters pass a toy cookie around the circle as you lead them in saying the chant. At the end of the chant, have the child with the cookie pretend to take a bite. Play several rounds.

Fresh from the oven, this cookie is hot!
Pass it around until it's not.
Too hot to eat and too hot to hold—
Pass it around till the cookie gets cold!

○ Have a child sit with her back to the group. In the center of the circle, place a cookie cutout on a plate. Prompt a classmate to take the cookie and conceal it. Ask, "Who took the cookie from the cookie plate?" Then have the child guess which classmate stole the cookie.

"Who took the cookie from the cookie plate?"

Center Time

○ **Fine Motor:** Provide craft foam circles, a supply of cotton rounds, and a paper plate. A student arranges the supplies so they resemble a plate full of sandwich cookies.

○ **Play Dough:** Place play dough and pieces of brown craft foam (chocolate chips) at a table. Also provide a rolling pin and a cookie tin. A child uses the materials to make chocolate chip cookies. Then he places the cookies in the tin.

○ **Math:** A student holds a handful of pom-poms (sprinkles) above a large cookie cutout and drops them. Then he counts the number of sprinkles that land on the cookie.

Songs and More

◯ Eat Them! ◯

(sung to the tune of "My Bonnie Lies Over the Ocean")

Some cookies are shaped like a circle.
Some cookies are shaped like a square.
Some cookies are shaped like a diamond.
I tell you I really don't care!
Eat them; eat them.
I'll eat any cookie I see, I see.
Eat them; eat them.
I'll eat any cookie I see!

◯ Cookies All Around ◯

Give each child a cookie cutout (patterns on page 20) and lead youngsters in reciting this action rhyme.

Cookies up.	*Hold cookie in the air.*
Cookies down.	*Hold cookie at your side.*
Cookies, cookies	
All around!	*Wave cookie all around.*
Cookie on your head.	*Hold cookie on your head.*
Cookie on your toes.	*Hold cookie on your toes.*
Cookie on your knees,	*Hold cookie on your knee.*
And cookie on your nose!	*Hold cookie on your nose.*

Storytime

◯ *If You Give a Mouse a Cookie*
by Laura Joffe Numeroff

◯ *Mr. Cookie Baker*
by Monica Wellington

◯ *Who Ate All the Cookie Dough?*
by Karen Beaumont

◯ *Who Stole the Cookies?*
by Judith Moffatt

Art

◯ Set out shallow containers of paint and textured cookies, such as chocolate sandwich cookies. Give each child a paper plate. Have her press a cookie in the paint and then onto the plate. Encourage her to repeat the process.

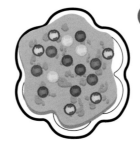

◯ Provide cookie cutouts (patterns on page 20), a mixture of light brown paint and dry oatmeal, and mini pompoms (sprinkles). Have a child paint a cookie with a thick layer of the mixture. Then encourage her to press sprinkles in the mixture.

Movement

◯ Divide the group into two equal lines. Give the first child in each line a paper plate with a cookie on it. On your signal, each student walks to a designated spot and back, hands the plate to the next player, and goes to the end of the line. Play continues until each child has a turn.

Transitions

◯ Play a quick question-and-answer game! For example, you might ask, "Would you rather eat a chocolate chip cookie or an oatmeal cookie?" Or ask a silly question like "Would you rather eat a meatball cookie or tuna fish cookie?" When a child answers, have him transition.

◯ Invite youngsters to make a pretend batch of kooky cookies! Ask each child to add a silly ingredient to an imaginary bowl of cookie batter. Have him "stir the batter" and then move to the next activity.

Cookie Patterns

Use with "Cookies All Around" and the second art activity on page 19.

TEC61354

TEC61354

TEC61354

TEC61354

Dinosaur Day

Circle Time

○ Ask a volunteer (parent dinosaur) to sit with her back to the group. Have her classmates pass a toy dinosaur around the circle as you say the rhyme. (Substitute "Dino dad" for a boy volunteer.) At the end of the rhyme, have the child with the toy roar like a baby dinosaur. Then have the parent dinosaur guess who has the baby.

> Dino mom, dino mom,
> Where'd your baby go?
> Dino mom, dino mom,
> Listen and you'll know!

○ Make dinosaur-related statements, such as "Some dinosaurs were very big" and "Dinosaurs wore clothes." When a statement is true, youngsters roar and stomp their big dinosaur feet. When a statement is false, they stay still.

Center Time

○ **Sand Table:** Bury toy dinosaurs and craft foam bones in the sand. Provide tweezers, a plastic shovel, paintbrushes, and a magnifying glass. A young paleontologist uses the tools to excavate, clean, and examine the artifacts he finds.

○ **Play Dough:** Provide play dough and small plastic dinosaurs. A child flattens a lump of dough; then she presses dinosaurs into the dough to make impressions.

○ **Writing:** Set out paper, assorted paper shapes, glue sticks, and markers. A student glues shapes to a sheet of paper to create his own unique dinosaur. Then he draws details and dictates a name and description of his dinosaur.

○ **Blocks:** Stock the area with toy dinosaurs, plastic eggs, blue paper (water), medium-size rocks, and silk plants. A youngster uses the blocks and props to create a prehistoric landscape. Then she engages in pretend dinosaur play.

○ See page 23 for a reproducible that targets fine-motor skills!

Songs and More

So Very Long Ago
(sung to the tune of "The Muffin Man")

Dinosaurs lived long ago,
So long ago, so long ago.
[Some were tall and some were small]
So very long ago!

Continue with the following: *Some moved fast and some moved slow; Some ate meat and some ate plants; Some liked water and some liked land; Some could fly and some could walk*

Storytime

○ *Edwina, the Dinosaur Who Didn't Know She Was Extinct* by Mo Willems

○ *If the Dinosaurs Came Back* by Bernard Most

○ *Dinosaur Roar!* by Paul Stickland

Art

○ Prepare a mixture of green paint and soil. Invite each child to paint an irregular-shaped paper cutout (swamp) with the mixture. Then invite him to walk a toy dinosaur through the swamp to create a trail of dinosaur footprints.

○ Have each child curl up on the floor pretending to be a baby dinosaur inside an egg. Prompt the babies to stretch, wiggle, arch their backs, and push their legs to "hatch" from their eggs. Then encourage them to walk, stomp, and squawk like baby dinosaurs.

Movement

○ Stand a distance from the group. Call out directions, such as "Take three giant dinosaur steps" or "Take six baby dinosaur steps," guiding students toward you. Periodically say, "Dinosaur roar!" prompting children to do their best dinosaur roar. Continue until youngsters reach you.

Dinosaur roar!

Transitions

○ Inspire critical thinking by asking questions such as, "If you were a really tall dinosaur, how could you be helpful?" or "If you were a dinosaur, how would you take a bath?" After a child shares his thoughts, have him move to the next activity.

More Fun

○ Hide several dinosaur books around the room. Tell students you brought dinosaur books to school but can't remember where you put them! Elicit their help in finding the books, and then read them throughout the day.

Dinosaurs

Just Hatched!

Note to the teacher: Invite a child to color the dinosaur on a copy of this page. Then have her use a white crayon to draw cracks on the egg, encouraging her to press down hard as she draws. Finally, have her paint the egg with watercolors to reveal the cracks.

Dr. Seuss Day

Circle Time

○ Give each child a green fried egg cutout and a yellow pom-pom (yolk). Chant, "Green eggs, green eggs, everywhere! Listen for a rhyming pair." Announce two words. If the words rhyme, youngsters place the yolk on the egg. If they do not, little ones hold their noses and say, "Stinky, stinky rotten eggs!"

○ Gather ten stackable items. Invite a student to stack the items as her classmates count them aloud. Then lead the group in chanting, "Ten [item name] up on top! Knock them over; see them drop!" prompting the child to knock the items over!

Center Time

○ **Play Dough:** Have a child use fish cookie cutters to make red and blue play dough fish. He says, "One fish, two fish, red fish, blue fish." Then he "feeds" the fish with an empty glitter shaker (fish food).

○ **Gross Motor:** Provide unbreakable items. A child pretends to be the Cat in the Hat and balances an item on her head. Then she attempts to walk across the area without the item falling off!

○ **Literacy:** Attach pairs of rhyming cards (see page 26) to pairs of footprint cutouts. After a read-aloud of *The Foot Book*, have students visit the center to match the rhyming pairs.

Songs and More

⃝ Up on Top ⃝

Stack ten felt apples on a flannelboard as you lead little ones in singing this song.

(sung to the tune of "Are You Sleeping?")

Stack one apple; stack two apples.
Now stack three; now stack four.
Stack five apples, five juicy apples,
Up on top! Up on top!

Stack six apples; stack seven apples.
Now stack eight; now stack nine.
Stack ten apples, ten juicy apples,
Up on top! Up on top!

⃝ How Do You Like That? ⃝

A fox in socks,
A cat in a hat,
A goat in a coat—
How do you like that?

A bear on a chair,
A rat on a bat,
A goose on a moose—
How do you like that?

Storytime

⃝ *Green Eggs and Ham*

⃝ *Ten Apples Up on Top!*

⃝ *One Fish Two Fish Red Fish Blue Fish*

⃝ *The Cat in the Hat*

⃝ *The Foot Book*

⃝ *Fox in Socks*

⃝ *There's a Wocket in My Pocket*

Snacktime

⃝ Have each child spoon a layer of blue gelatin into a disposable cup and then add two fish crackers, encouraging her to chant "one fish, two fish, [color name] fish, [color name] fish!" Have her repeat the process to complete her snack.

Art

⃝ Place a fried egg cutout in a box. Have a child dip a plastic egg in green paint and place it in the box. Then encourage him to use a spatula to roll the egg around. Have him remove the egg and attach a yellow pom-pom yolk.

Movement

⃝ Have students (fish) stand side by side. Stand a distance away with your back to them. Instruct the fish to "swim" toward you as you say, "One fish, two fish, please don't move fish!" and then stop at the end of the chant. Turn around to "catch" any fish still swimming; then pull each one out of the water with an imaginary fishing pole and have her swim to the back of the group. Play several rounds.

Transition

⃝ Use *Green Eggs and Ham* as food for thought during this transition activity! Ask each child to name a green food before moving on. If he can't think of one, have him name a different-color food he would eat if it was green, like green mashed potatoes!

More Fun

⃝ After reading *There's a Wocket in My Pocket*, draw and cut out a few simple creatures and attach them to specific items in your room, such as the clock and the door. On occasion throughout the day, direct youngsters' attention to a creature. For example, you might say, "Oh my goodness, there's a flock on the clock!"

Rhyming Cards

Use with the literacy center on page 24.

TEC61354

TEC61354

TEC61354

TEC61354

TEC61354

TEC61354

TEC61354

TEC61354

TEC61354

TEC61354

TEC61354

TEC61354

Duck Day

Circle Time

Have little ones pass a rubber duck (or yellow pom-pom) around the circle as you lead them in singing the song. When the song ends, the child holding the duck says, "Quack, quack!"

(sung to the tune of the chorus of "Jingle Bells")

Little duck, little duck
Going round and round.
When the song comes to an end,
Please make a quacking sound!

Invite a child to roll a large die and count the dots aloud. Then have the group quack that many times, guiding them by holding up one finger for each quack.

Center Time

Play Dough: Provide yellow play dough and craft feathers, orange tagboard rectangles (beaks), mini pom-poms (eyes), and blue laminated pond shapes (or vinyl placemats). A child uses the materials to make a duck. Then he pretends the duck is swimming in a pond.

Water Table: Float rubber ducks in the water. Provide a squirt bottle filled with water. A youngster squirts each duck to maneuver it through the water, quacking each time she pulls the bottle's trigger.

Fine Motor: Fill a tub with brown paper shreds so it resembles a nest. Add plastic eggs containing yellow pom-poms (ducklings). A student opens each egg, pretending the ducklings are hatching, and says, "Peep, peep!" as he plays. Then he puts each duckling back in its egg and seals it closed.

Songs and More

○ Waddle, Waddle ○

Have your little ducklings waddle behind you as you lead them in singing this song.

(sung to the tune of "Are You Sleeping?")

Little ducklings, little ducklings
In a row, in a row.
See the ducklings waddle,
See the ducklings waddle
To and fro, to and fro.

○ Silly Duck! ○

A duck plays in the rain or sun.
A duck flies over everyone.
It gets its food while upside down.
That duck is such a silly clown!

Art

○ Have each child glue torn blue tissue paper strips (water) to a sheet of paper. Then have her glue a duck cutout (pattern on page 29) to the water. Encourage her to glue yellow craft feathers to the duck and draw desired details.

○ Set out a shallow container of orange paint. Provide a spatula, green crinkle shreds (grass), and glue. Have a child dip the spatula in the paint and press it on a large sheet of paper so it resembles a webbed footprint. After making several prints, encourage her to glue grass around the prints.

Movement

○ Encourage youngsters to follow along as you perform duck-inspired sound and action patterns, such as "quack, quack, flap;" "flap, flap, fly;" and "waddle, waddle, quack."

○ Place blue bulletin board paper (pond) on the floor. Direct your little ducks to quietly waddle around the pond. After a few moments say, "Quack, quack!" signaling the ducks to waddle into the pond and "swim" around, quacking as they swim. Repeat as desired.

Quack, quack!

Transitions

○ Recite this adorable rhyme to settle little ones in for naptime.

Waddle like a duck as you go to your place.
Flap your wings when you get to your space.
Sit like a duck in a cozy nest.
Now lay down for a ducky rest.

○ Try this fun idea to transition the group to or from the classroom! Have students line up behind you. Introduce yourself as Mama Duck and instruct your little ducklings to imitate your actions. Then waddle, flap, "swim," and "fly" as you move along.

Songs and More

○ Splendid Seasons ○
(sung to the tune of the chorus of "Jingle Bells")

Summertime, wintertime,
Springtime, and the fall—
These are the four seasons.
What's your favorite one of all?

Summertime, wintertime,
Springtime, and the fall—
These are the four seasons.
What's your favorite one of all?

○ Food Favorites ○
(sung to the tune of "This Old Man")

Of the foods
That we eat,
Which foods are a favorite treat?
Will you name a food that you enjoy a bunch?
Name one that you love to munch.

Snacktime

○ Provide cookies and a sampling of milk flavors, such as chocolate, strawberry, and plain. Encourage youngsters to taste each type of milk as they eat their cookie snack. Then have each child vote for her favorite milk!

Art

○ Set out collage materials and paper in a variety of colors. Invite each child to choose his favorite color paper. Then encourage him to make a collage using his favorite color craft materials. Personalize his work with a tag that says "[Child's name]'s favorite color is [color name]!"

○ Have each child glue a crumpled piece of tissue paper in a bowl to represent her favorite ice cream flavor. Invite her to drizzle glue on the tissue paper and then sprinkle her favorite candy sprinkles on the glue. Finally, have her add a plastic spoon to the bowl.

Movement

○ Announce directions for youngsters to follow, such as the following: If your favorite color is green, touch your toes five times. If your favorite ice cream is chocolate, hop like a bunny. If your favorite toy is a doll, spin around.

○ Invite a child to mimic his favorite animal and have his classmates follow suit.

○ Invite students, in turn, to stand in front of the group as you lead the class in chanting "Please show us your favorite move so we can do it too!" Then encourage the child to demonstrate a motion for her classmates to perform.

Transition

○ Choose a different favorite to spotlight during each transition. For example, you might say, "If your favorite weather is rainy weather, please line up."

My favorite memory is...

by _____

Frog Day

Circle Time

Have each little frog hold a blowout party blower (frog tongue) and hop around as you recite the rhyme. During the final line, have the frogs flick out their tongues to "catch a fly."

Little frogs with hopping feet,
Searching for some flies to eat.
Hungry froggies hopping by
Stop and try to catch a fly!

Stage the room with green items. Display a green toy frog and ask, "What do you think a frog's favorite color could be?" After determining that it could be green, ask each student to find one green item. Then have each child identify her item and place it by the frog.

Center Time

Math: Set out brown paper strips (logs), frog counters, and a large die. A student rolls the die, counts the dots, and "hops" that many frogs onto a log. After each player has a turn, students compare the number of frogs on each log.

Sensory: Fill a tub with green paper shreds. Hide large green pom-poms (frogs) in the shreds. Place a paper lily pad nearby. A child searches for frogs, saying "ribbit, ribbit" as he works. He places each frog he finds on the lily pad and then counts the frogs in his collection.

Fine Motor: Attach a toy frog (or a green pom-pom) to a spring-style clothespin. Set out black pom-poms (flies) and an empty bowl. A youngster uses the clothespin to "catch" each fly and drop it in the bowl.

Songs and More

⬤ Time for Lunch! ⬤

Frog sits quietly on a log,
Waiting for some lunch.
Flick goes his sticky tongue.
And then it's time to munch!

Frog rolls up his sticky tongue
To munch his tasty treat.
When he's done, he quietly waits
For something else to eat!

⬤ Frisky Frogs ⬤

Invite your little frogs to move around a blue paper pond as you sing this fun action song!

(sung to the tune of "For He's a Jolly Good Fellow")

See all the speckled frogs [hopping].　　*Hop around the pond.*
See all the speckled frogs [hopping].
See all the speckled frogs [hopping]—
[Hopping] around the pond! Splash!　　*Jump in the pond on "splash."*

Continue with the following: *walking, marching, crawling, tiptoeing, side-stepping*

Art

⬤ Mix together green paint, sand, and glue. Have youngsters paint a thick layer of the mixture on a tagboard frog (pattern on page 35) and then press jumbo wiggle eyes on the frog.

Snacktime

⬤ Have each child spread green-tinted whipped cream cheese on a rice cake. Then have her add two cucumber slices (eyes), two chocolate chips (pupils), and a strawberry slice (tongue). For added fun, invite her to put a chocolate chip (fly) on the tongue!

Movement

⬤ Use sidewalk chalk to draw lily pad shapes on an outdoor surface. Label each shape with a symbol, such as a number, letter, or shape. Then call out a symbol, prompting your little frogs to hop to the designated lily pad.

⬤ Place a gray rock cutout on the floor. Invite one of your little frogs to jump off the rock. Then use die-cut frogs to measure how far he jumped!

⬤ Position a long brown paper strip (log) on the floor and a plastic bug (or large pom-pom) a short distance away. Invite a few youngsters (frogs) to leap from the log toward the bug. Repeat the activity, moving the bug farther away from the log each time.

Transitions

⬤ Attach a path of lily pad cutouts leading to your circle-time area. As each child transitions to or from circle time, have her hop from one lily pad to the next, encouraging her to count the lily pads as she hops.

⬤ Encourage little ones to pretend they are frogs hopping from one destination to the next!

More Fun

⬤ Partially hide a frog cutout (pattern on page 35) somewhere in the room. Tell youngsters to be on the lookout for the hidden frog. When a child spots the frog, she says, "Ribbit, ribbit!" and then reveals its location. Secretly move the frog throughout the day and continue the search.

Ladybug Day

Circle Time

○ Set out a large spot-free ladybug cutout labeled with letters. Name a letter; then invite a volunteer to place a chocolate sandwich cookie atop the letter. When all the letters are covered, hand out cookie treats!

○ Give each child a leaf cutout and a red pom-pom (ladybug). Then lead little ones in some lively ladybug fun by having each child "crawl" her ladybug above, below, around, on top of, and under the leaf. For an added challenge, give directions that include two positional words.

Center time

○ **Math:** Provide spot-free ladybug cutouts, black checkers (spots), and a large die. In turn, each child rolls the die, counts the dots, and then places that many spots on her ladybug. After each player has a turn, students compare the number of spots on each ladybug.

○ **Sensory:** Hide ten red pom-poms (ladybugs) in a plastic tub filled with green paper shreds. Punch ten holes in a paper leaf and place it nearby. A child digs through the shreds to find the ladybugs. He puts each one he finds atop a hole in the leaf and says, "Munch, munch, munch!"

○ **Literacy:** Cut out the cards on page 41 and place them facedown near a red ink pad. Give each child a leaf cutout. Each student flips a card and names the picture. If the name begins with /l/, each child makes a red thumbprint on his leaf. After all the cards are flipped, youngsters draw ladybug details on each print.

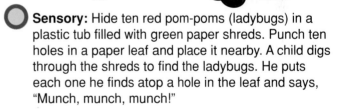

Songs and More

○ Ladybugs ○
(sung to the tune of "Are You Sleeping?")

Ladybugs, ladybugs,
Watch them crawl. They're so small!
They will munch and crunch
Aphids for their lunch.
Ladybugs, ladybugs.

○ Sweet Dreams, Ladybugs ○

Ladybugs, ladybugs, on the ground,
Ladybugs, ladybugs, crawl around.
Ladybugs, ladybugs, not a peep!
Ladybugs, ladybugs, go to sleep.

Get on hands and knees.
Slowly crawl around.
Stay still and silent.
Curl up and pretend to sleep.

Storytime

○ *The Grouchy Ladybug*
by Eric Carle

○ *The Very Lazy Ladybug*
by Isobel Finn

○ *Ten Little Ladybugs*
by Melanie Gerth

Art

○ To make this ladybug masterpiece, dip the edge of a wide foam brush in green paint and gently dab it on paper so the dabs resemble blades of grass. Next, dip one end of a cork in red paint and press it on the paper to make ladybug bodies.

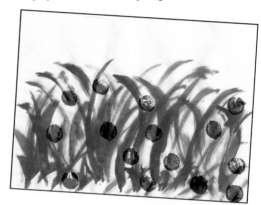

Snacktime

○ Have each youngster spread red-tinted whipped cream cheese on a mini bagel half. Then have her add chocolate chip eyes and spots along with pretzel stick halves for antennae.

Movement

○ Help the group stand in two equal lines. Place a leaf cutout a distance from each line. Give each child a pom-pom (ladybug). In relay fashion, each child crawls to his team's leaf, puts his ladybug on it, and then crawls to the end of the line. Continue until all the ladybugs are on the leaves.

○ Place a large flower cutout on the floor. Mark a start line a few feet from the flower and place two or three red pom-poms (ladybugs) on the line. Have a different child kneel behind each ladybug. On your signal, each youngster blows on her ladybug until it rests on the flower.

○ Have little ones get on all fours and pretend to be ladybugs. Stand a distance from the group. Say, "Ladybugs on the move!" signaling youngsters to crawl toward you. Then say, "Ladybugs rest!" prompting children to stop. Continue until all the ladybugs reach you.

TEC61354

TEC61354

TEC61354

TEC61354

TEC61354

TEC61354

TEC61354

TEC61354

TEC61354

TEC61354

TEC61354

TEC61354

Luau Day

Circle Time

Try this fun version of Hot Potato called Crack the Coconut! Play a recording of music and have little ones pass a coconut (or a paper cutout) around the circle. Stop the music and have the child holding the coconut tell how he would crack it open. Then restart the music and continue the activity.

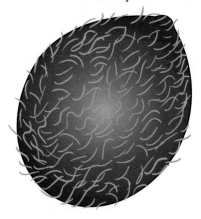

Display several real or plastic tropical fruits. Review the fruits with students; then have them close their eyes. Hide a fruit from view and chant, "Tropical fruit tastes yum, yum, yum! One is missing; can you tell which one?" Then have students open their eyes and name the missing fruit.

Center Time

Discovery: Set out an assortment of tropical fruit. Also provide a magnifying glass, a scale, and a cloth tape measure (or a length of yarn for nonstandard measurement). A student uses the tools to examine, weigh, and measure the fruit.

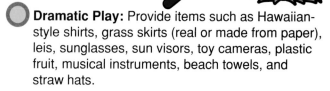

Dramatic Play: Provide items such as Hawaiian-style shirts, grass skirts (real or made from paper), leis, sunglasses, sun visors, toy cameras, plastic fruit, musical instruments, beach towels, and straw hats.

Play Dough: Set out brown and white coconut-scented play dough along with a toy hammer and a plastic knife. A child rolls a ball of white dough and then wraps it with brown dough, sniffing the scent as he works. He taps the "coconut" with the hammer, pretending to break it open. Then he cuts it in half.

See page 44 for a reproducible that targets fine-motor skills!

Songs and More

◯ A-L-O-H-A! ◯

Explain to little ones that *aloha* is a Hawaiian greeting that means *hello* or *goodbye*. Then lead them in practicing the greeting with this fun song! Repeat the verse, replacing *hello* with *goodbye*.

(sung to the tune of "Bingo")

There is a way to say [hello].
Aloha is the way, oh!
A-L-O-H-A,
A-L-O-H-A,
A-L-O-H-A.
Aloha is the way, oh!

◯ Hula Dance ◯
(sung to the tune of "Where Is Thumbkin?")

Hula dance,
Hula dance,
Sway your hips,
Sway your hips!
That is what you do.
Aloha to you!
Hula dance,
Hula dance.

Snacktime

◯ Set out several kinds of sliced tropical fruit, individual condiment cups filled with vanilla yogurt, and paper plates. Invite a child to place desired fruit on his plate. Then encourage him to use the yogurt as dipping sauce for his fruit. Tasty!

Art

◯ Dip a lei in a shallow container of paint and "dance" it across a sheet of paper. Repeat the process with other leis and colors of paint.

◯ Color paper cupcake liners with markers or crayons. Then tape the liners to a length of yarn. Hang this lovely flower garland as a festive decoration!

Movement

◯ Arrange several toy hoops in a circle on the floor. Gather a number of students equal to the number of hoops and have them walk around the hoops. After a few moments, start some music, signaling each child to hop in a hoop and hula dance! Stop the music and continue in the same way for several rounds.

◯ Put on some lively music and have an assistant help you hold a broomstick limbo-stick style. Then invite each child to limbo under the stick!

Transitions

◯ Say *aloha* to greet youngsters in the morning and to dismiss them at the end of the day. Or sing the first song above.

◯ To incorporate movement with your transitions, have youngsters hula to their chosen centers!

◯ Play a recording of soothing tropical music to help little ones settle in for naptime.

Crack That Coconut!

Preschool Fun Days • ©The Mailbox® Books • TEC61354

Note to the teacher: Have a child use a mixture of brown paint and sand to paint the coconut on a copy of this page. Then have her press pieces of brown embroidery thread or thin brown yarn into the wet mixture. Invite her to color the remainder of the page.

Monster Day

BOO!

Circle Time

○ Invite youngsters to describe what a monster might look like if it were real. Encourage students to use lots of descriptive language to aid you in drawing the monster they describe.

○ Display a drawing of a monster head, minus the mouth. Blindfold a volunteer and encourage her to attach a mouth cutout to the head. Then have students use positional words to describe where she put the mouth. For example, the mouth could be *above* the eyes, *beside* the head, *under* an ear, or *on* the nose!

Center Time

○ **Fine Motor:** Provide a supersize monster head, minus hair. Youngsters snip yarn into small pieces and then glue the pieces to the monster to make hair.

○ **Play Dough:** Set out play dough and a variety of craft items. A youngster uses the dough and craft items to create her own unique monster.

○ **Math:** Provide assorted-size monster footprints (pattern on page 47) and linking cubes. A child chooses a footprint, snaps together cubes to match the length of the foot, and then counts the cubes.

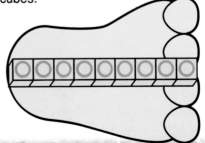

Songs and More

○ There's No Such Thing as Monsters ○

Lead youngsters in singing this song. Then invite each child to tell about a time she was scared by a noise she thought was a monster, like a cat playing under a bed!

(sung to the tune of "Did You Ever See a Lassie? ")

If there's no such thing as monsters,
As monsters, as monsters,
If there's no such thing as monsters,
What's that noise that I hear?

It's rumbling and grumbling.
It's rumbling and grumbling.
If there's no such thing as monsters,
What's that noise that I hear?

○ Scary Monster! ○

I am a monster—see my paws!	*Hold up hands.*
I'll stomp, stomp, stomp	*Stomp.*
And show my claws!	*Spread fingers.*
I'll bare my teeth	*Bare teeth.*
And scratch my fur.	*Scratch side.*
And then I'll growl a great big "Grrrr!"	*Strike a scary pose.*

Art

○ Give each child a folded paper plate. Have her unfold the plate and drizzle paint on one half. Help her refold the plate; then have her rub her hand across it. Have her unfold the plate; then use assorted craft materials to create monsterlike details.

○ Set out white paint thickened with flour (or potato flakes) and a potato masher. Play a recording of "Monster Mash" or another monster-related tune while youngsters gently mash the "potatoes" and then press the masher on a sheet of colored paper to make mashed-potato prints.

Transition

○ Instruct each student to pretend to be a tiny monster, a giant monster, a swimming monster, or a flying monster as she transitions from one activity to another.

More Fun

○ For more musical fun, transform traditional songs to match your monster theme. For example, transform "The Itsy-Bitsy Spider" into "The Itsy-Bitsy Monster" or "Ten Little Indians" into "Ten Little Monsters."

Storytime

○ *Leonardo the Terrible Monster*
by Mo Willems

○ *Go Away Big Green Monster!*
by Ed Emberly

○ *If You're a Monster and You Know It*
by Rebecca Emberly and Ed Emberly

Snacktime

○ Have each child spread frosting on a sugar cookie. Then have him create his own cookie monster by adding items such as cereal, miniature chocolate chips, pretzel sticks, and M&M's Minis candies.

Movement

○ Play a recording of "The Purple People Eater" or "Monster Mash" and direct little ones to dance and stomp using their big monster feet. Stop the music, prompting each child to hold his monster pose. Restart the music and continue until the song ends.

Terrific Treasure!

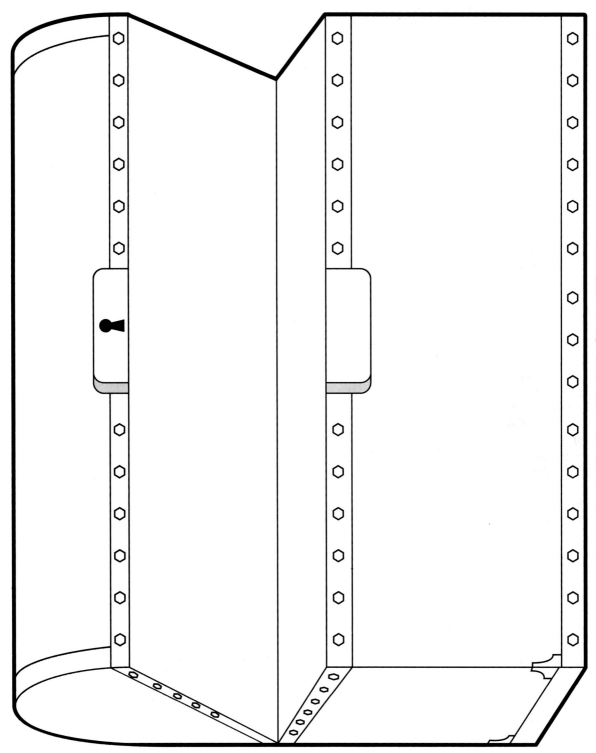

Note to the teacher: Use with the literacy center on page 61 and the first art activity on page 62.

63

Pocket Day

Circle Time

Help each youngster place a linking cube (or something similar) in each of her pockets. Have her count her pockets, remove the cubes from her pockets, and then count the cubes. Then have her snap the cubes together and compare the length with that of a partner's cubes.

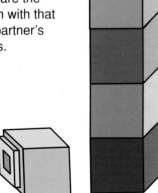

Conceal an item in one of your pockets. Then provide clues leading little ones to guess the identity of the hidden object. Repeat with a variety of items.

Center Time

Play Dough: Invite students to make pockets from colorful play dough. Provide items such as animal figurines and plastic counters that can be put in and taken out of the pockets.

Discovery: Place items to investigate in the individual pockets of a shoe or jewelry organizer. Items might include a feather, a clump of moss, tree bark, a magnet, a wind-up toy, and so on.

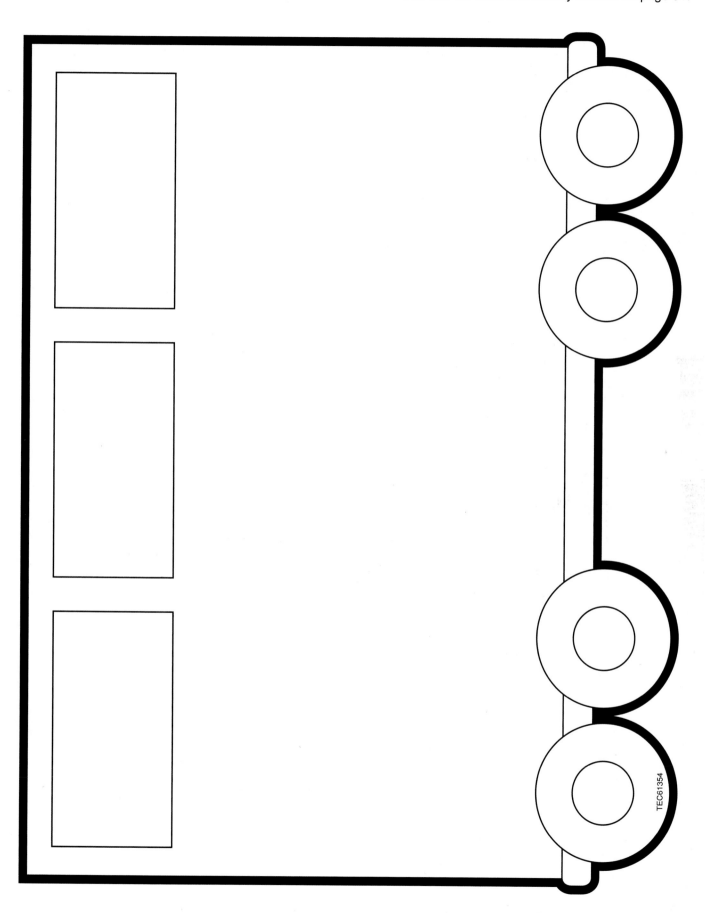

TEC61354

Western Day

Circle Time

○ Cut out copies of the cow pattern on page 96 and scatter the cutouts around the room. Time youngsters as they "herd" the cows by picking them up and placing them in a specified location. Repeat the activity and have little ones try to beat their time.

○ Play a recording of music as students carefully pass a bowl of dried beans around the circle. Stop the music and encourage the child with the beans to strike a triangle and say, "Chowtime!" Continue for several rounds.

Center Time

○ **Dramatic Play:** Provide cowboy hats and boots, plaid shirts, and bandanas. If desired, also add a mock campfire, ropes, tote bags (saddle bags), and plastic cups and plates. Youngsters use the items for imaginary play!

○ **Blocks:** Bend pipe cleaners so they resemble lassos and place them at the center along with toy farm animals. Students lasso the animals and then use the blocks to create pens for them.

○ **Fine Motor:** Provide a variety of uncooked pasta and cutout copies of the boot pattern on page 96. A child decorates a boot by gluing dyed pasta to it. Now that's fancy!

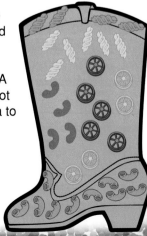

Songs and More

◯ Get Dressed! ◯

Have each child touch his head, waist, thighs, and feet during the third through fifth lines of this song!

(sung to the tune of "Bingo")

The cowboy dresses for his ride,
And this is how he does it.
Hat, belt, chaps, and boots!
Hat, belt, chaps, and boots!
Hat, belt, chaps, and boots!
And this is how he does it.

◯ Cows and Chow ◯

(sung to the tune of "If You're Happy and You Know It")

Let's all ride our little horses round the ranch. Yee-haw!
Let's all ride our little horses round the ranch. Yee-haw!
We will rope a little cow
And then go back and have some chow!
Let's all ride our little horses round the ranch. Yee-haw!

Snacktime

◯ Give each child a lunch-size paper bag trimmed as shown so it resembles a saddlebag. Have her place a mixture of cereal pieces, pretzels, and M&M's Minis candies in the bag. Then fold down the top and secure it with a colorful sticky dot.

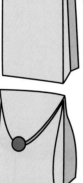

Art

◯ Trim sponges into horseshoe shapes and place each one near a shallow pan of paint. A child makes horseshoe prints on a sheet of paper.

◯ Give each child a white handkerchief. Encourage her to paint on the handkerchief with fabric paint to make her own bandana!

Movement

◯ Give each child a length of yarn (rattlesnake). When you shake a maraca, encourage students to wiggle their snakes on the floor. When you stop playing, have students hold their snakes still.

◯ Designate one side of the room for cowgirls and the opposite side for cowboys. Have students dance (or gallop) to a country western music recording. Say, "Round 'em up!" prompting the cowgirls and cowboys to go to the correct sides of the room. Repeat the activity.

◯ Have students pretend they are riding horses, encouraging them to walk, trot, gallop, and jump.

Transitions

◯ Choose a child to pretend to be a cowboy. The remaining youngsters pretend to be cows wandering about the classroom. A child gallops to each cow and touches her on the shoulder. As soon as a cow is touched, she gets in line.

◯ To transition to naptime, tell students that cowboys would sing to the herd at night to calm them. Have students pretend to be cows as they settle down for naptime. Then quietly play a music recording of soothing folksongs.

Cow Pattern
Use with the first circle-time idea on page 94.

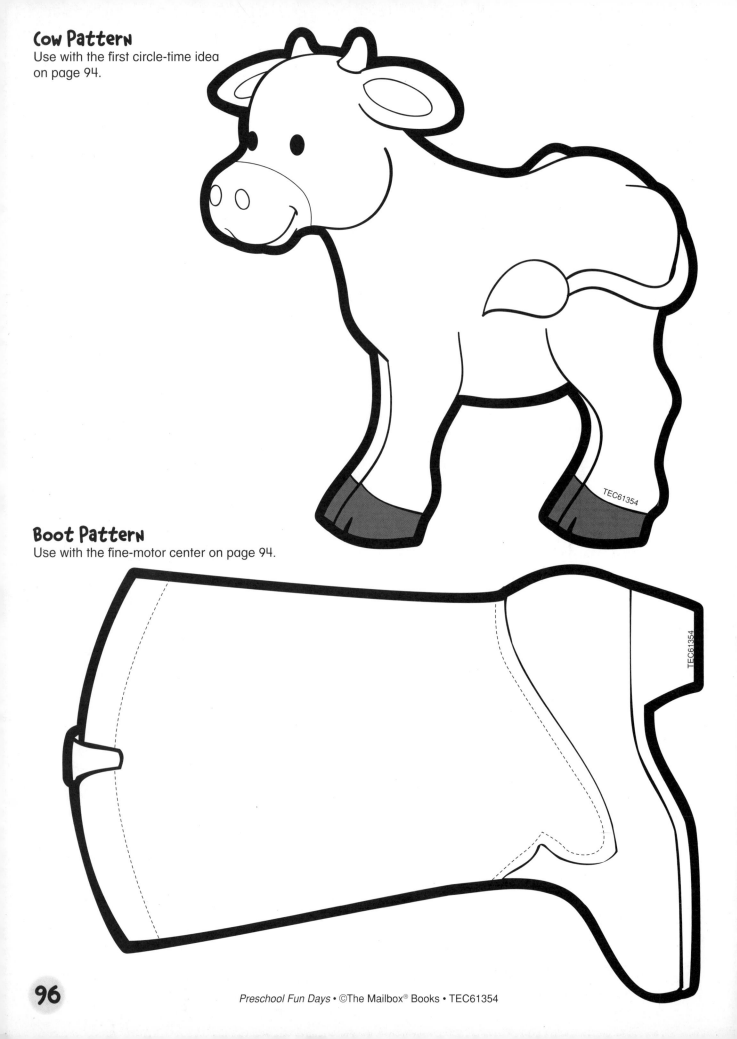

TEC61354

Boot Pattern
Use with the fine-motor center on page 94.

TEC61354